MW00712407

Twenty First Century Pilgrim

Roam to Rome

The Long-Distance Ramblings of Peter Shackleton

By
Peter Shackleton
and
Heather Russell

RUSSHACK PRESS
12 Newcroft Close
Hillingdon Middlesex UB8 3RJ

First published by Russhack Press 2008
Copyright Peter Shackleton 2008

ISBN: 978-0-9561139-0-0

Set in Gill Sans MT
By Russhack Press and printed in Great Britain
by Cpod, Wiltshire

Contents

A light-hearted look at the 1300 mile walk from Clifford, just north of Hay on Wye, all the way to Rome. The ups and downs of the weather, the people, scenery, wildlife, flora and fauna and the ups and downs of the Alps, all are here as seen from the 'glass half full' viewpoint of Peter - and the lens of the camera.

Dedication

Custom and tradition require that every book must have a dedication and complying is indeed every author's pleasure. The difficulty for this volume arises in selecting the recipients of the dedication.

From my early childhood my family travelled almost every weekend, and for the duration of all school holidays, to often remote areas of southern England with our 16 foot touring caravan. In the 1950s, for a working class family in the small west London suburb of Southall, this was most unusual. My parents, therefore, should probably be at the top of my 'travel bug' dedication list.

Since the 1970s I have enjoyed the privilege of venturing many thousands of miles, to some very interesting locations, alongside my friends with disabilities in Hillingdon.
They, and their dedicated scores of supporting volunteers, are next.

Andy Johnson must be credited for bringing out the walker in me as, before I met him, I usually tackled any journey in excess of a couple of miles by some form of motorised transport. He, then takes his place on the list.

Over the last forty five years, since leaving school at 15, I've been blessed with a veritable host of supportive personal friends who have encouraged and assisted me in everything I've done. By far too numerous to list without risking missing out someone vital, they know well who they are. They all take their rightful places here.

So, at the end of this preamble, I have had to select just three particularly inspiring people to appear on the following page.

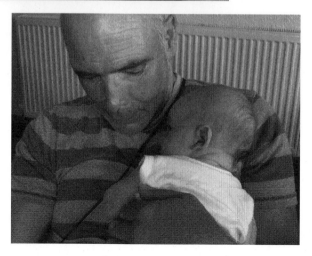

They are:

Mike Harris
1952 - 2008
My travelling companion up in the frighteningly fast lift of
the World Trade Center,
the steep and slippery footpath beside Niagara Falls,
down a Swiss cave,
and many pubs, restaurants and 747s on the way.

MJ Nuqui
Who has generously forgiven me for missing both his
Christening and his first birthday whilst rambling this road.

Matti Ager
Who, at just six and a half weeks old, brought his
mother and father down from Hertfordshire to Portsmouth
to wave us 'Bon Voyage'

Introduction

Often, when getting started on almost any kind of difficult or lengthy project, many people will take a deep breath, sigh, then say:

"A journey of a thousand miles starts with a single step."

This is actually very seldom true.

Journeys of any length, from as short as popping down the road to the shops, to - well - trekking a thousand miles or more, always take some degree of planning and forethought. Going to the shops without the necessary means to pay for your purchase would be a rather short-sighted exercise, especially if you did so without ensuring the house was safe and secure for your return (and you'd taken the key!). Similarly, the long distance trek shared with you in this volume did not start with that moment of the first step, but sometime rather earlier.

Andy Johnson and I have walked together frequently since we first became friends in the early 1990's. Notable amongst these were unsuccessfully attempting to cross Wales east to west in 1995, successfully crossing Wales west to east in 1996, rambling around chunks of Australia in 1997, crossing the Himalaya from Nepal into Tibet in 1999, England to Santiago in 2004 and Offa's Dyke in 2006. All these trips needed discussing, planning the time and finance and agreeing the general principles before that first step could be taken. For some, suitable and similarly crazy friends were also needed.

The idea that we'd quite like to tackle the road to Rome was born mostly out of the fulfilment gained from our 2004 hike to Santiago in northern Spain.

Andy started that one from his home in Herefordshire - I started from the Mencap Social Centre in Hillingdon, west London. Our routes converged at our friend Alice's home in Andover. The reason for the split start was that Andy wanted to fulfil his 'Laurie Lee' dream to take a very long walk from his own front door, and I was being sponsored in aid of double glazing the social centre. We both thoroughly enjoyed the Santiago pilgrimage trail and decided almost before completion that we'd like to tackle another one, and the sponsorship brought in a full quarter of the re-glazing costs. In the intervening four years between Santiago and Rome we both selected worthwhile charities we wanted to support, and Andy became partnered with Karen.

Andy's selected charity for this trip was Amnesty International, mine the Friends and Supporters of the St. Owen's Centre in Hereford. Details of these two organisations and Mencap Hillingdon South, the beneficiaries of the 2004 trek, can be found on pages 84-86

2008 also seemed like a good year for me to tackle an adventure like this as it was the year I attained 60, started drawing a small pension, and was issued with my Freedom [bus] Pass.

Peter Shackleton

The beginning

<u>Thursday 1st May</u>

So here I am, stepping out from the front door on the morning of my day one, full of the joy of freedom that the start of any adventure brings. On the mantleshelf behind me are thoughtful cards from friends wishing 'Bon Voyage' and taking the first picture is my good friend Sharon who, with the help of her family, will keep a watchful neighbourly eye on the cottage whilst I'm away. The sun is shining brightly as I head along the disused railway towards Whitney Toll Bridge and my first opportunity for 'en route' sponsorship. I engage the plan that I used with success on my way to Santiago. I start the conversation by asking the man collecting the tolls to guess where I am going with the promise that if he guesses correctly I'll give him five pounds. Having explained my sponsorship intentions I then ask if he is incorrect would he sponsor me the five pounds. The ensuing conversation nets the funds ten pounds and I leave with a spring in my step. Two more encounters brought a further seven pounds and I arrive at Andy and Karen's home feeling quite content.

| Logaston | ⟶ | 19 miles | ⟵ | Hereford |
| Hereford | | 19½ miles | | Hollybush |

Friday 2nd May

After a comfortable night at Logaston, Andy, Karen and I are accompanied on the journey to Hereford by those members of the Almeley Walking group who don't need to work on Fridays! We reach Hereford with only one light shower, but more are forecast for the weekend. Another comfortable night, this time staying with our friend Chris near the city centre. Always plenty to eat here with a serious danger of the quality and size of the meals interfering with our ability to walk anywhere.

Saturday 3rd May

We have our official start from the Cathedral Green at 8.30am. We are given a great send off with gifts of pilgrim shells from the Cathedral and interviews by the Hereford Times. Among the sizeable gathering of family and friends supporting us this morning are Sandie, Anita, Gina, Gary and Sarala - staff, friends and supporters of St. Owens - all suitably dressed for today's walk to Hollybush. Gary also has his overnight backpack as he is generously released by his wife and children to give us two full days' encouragement and companionship. After a pleasant chatty day's walk involving the full range of border counties weather, and having bade farewell to most of our larger group, Gary, Andy, Karen and I arrive at the bunkhouse at Hollybush where we are all accommodated in one room. Andy and Karen head off to dine with local friends whilst Gary and I create a culinary delight from a couple of supermarket packets. Having consumed our gourmet feast we are joined by three generations of my extended family who are spending the bank holiday weekend at Clifford, and have come along in their car to take us to the pub. A very pleasant end to an enjoyable day.

Sunday 4th - Monday 5th May

Up with the lark we set off in good spirits for the 23 mile walk to Cheltenham. This is accomplished using footpaths and minor roads, crossing the Severn at Tirley. On the outskirts of town we bid farewell and thanks to Gary, then trudge through the industrial and superstore area north-west of Cheltenham, the town centre, then a further couple of miles out to the east. We are greeted by Julian and Charlotte, Andy's relatives, who have kindly agreed to accommodate us. Here we have our first scheduled rest day on bank holiday Monday and the two overnights that entails. Julian, Charlotte and the girls only moved house just one week before we arrived, so builders and decorators are still about. Andy and Karen get the one completed guest room and I am on the sofa. All three of us enjoy the luxury of soaking our aching muscles in the bath, but only Andy is caught on camera!

Tuesday 6th May

Andy's map now leads us almost due south, again minor roads and footpaths bringing us eventually to the camping and caravan site Mayfield Park, Cirencester, on the A435. Our hosts here are the proprietors Peter and June with Adrian and Jan. They let us camp free *and* sponsor us. We enjoy the on-site take-away catering, a lovely fresh rhubarb crumble and our first night of real camping.

Wednesday 7th May

Another pleasant day's walking brings us to the Second Chance Campsite beside the shallow end of the Thames at Castle Eaton. A few blisters are irritating us all now, but we are still going well. Knowing it was likely to be very hot today we had an early start, so after our short evening stroll to the pub we settle down for an early night with the sounds of the trickling Thames and its associated wildlife to lull us to sleep.

Thursday 8th May

To reach Mildenhall east of Marlborough we walk 23 miles today circling Swindon using countless awkward and overgrown stiles. We cross the Swindon to London main railway line (*carefully, there's no bridge!*) and the M4, then climb up along the Ridgeway path. We arrive at the Church Farm campsite at 6.00pm, just as the church clock strikes. Having started at 7.15am, we are tired and ready for dinner at the pub! Somewhere along the way the first 100 mile barrier is broken today.

Friday 9th May

Today's journey towards Andover takes us through the beautiful and seemingly timeless Savernake Forest, and among some of the oldest surviving trees in the country. We are grateful for its leafy shade as the clouds have cleared and the sunlit un-shaded paths before and beyond the forest are almost unbearably hot. We reach the Wyke Down campsite mid afternoon, pitch tents, shower and wash our clothes then eat in the site's own busy restaurant.

Saturday 10th - Monday 12th May

Following the straight old Roman road as much as possible we arrive in Winchester a bit footsore and weary. Over 120 miles completed so we get another day off tomorrow (Sunday) for good behaviour!! Bluebells and wildlife in the woods today are really wonderful and discovering an 'away from the traffic' footpath existing alongside the main road into the city is a really pleasant surprise. Sunday 11th is a leisurely day off spent relaxing, shopping for changes and improvements to bits of our kit, and drinking copious amounts of tea. An evening at the theatre being entertained by Jo Brand rounds off our mini break. Our friend Andy A's hospitality is first class as usual. Monday 12th and there is familiar ground beneath our feet now as we are following the same route to Portsmouth that Andy and I followed in 2004. We know there's no campsite at our destination village of Droxford, halfway between Winchester and Portsmouth, but we do know there are a couple of good pubs to choose from for our evening meal. The church porch, though open to the elements at one end, provides a dry flat surface on which we roll out our sleeping bags. The more permanent residents in the churchyard don't seem to mind.

<u>Tuesday 13th May</u>

Familiar ground again today as we complete the English leg of the journey in warm sunshine. The heat is giving us a few leg problems so we are a bit slow today but getting there! The ferry sails at 11.00pm, so we are taking a more leisurely stroll than usual. We have a very pleasant late afternoon spent with our youngest sponsor Matti Ager, here with his Mum Rhia and Dad Oly to wave us off. After this we have no more time off for about 10 days so are thankful for an

easier day like today. Karen visits Millets to get me the smaller, lighter tent which I phoned from Winchester to reserve, and returns with a new smart sunhat as well. Our friends take the heavier tent home with them as we make our way to the Portsmouth ferry terminal to check in. Have collected a few more sponsors along the way.

Wednesday 14th May

What a day we have today. Arriving at Le Havre at 8.00am we are taken off the ferry to the terminal by bus, shunted through a maze of glass passageways to passport control only to find it locked and closed. Pushing open the fire escape to exit the building and setting off the alarm system, we walk out of the port unchallenged except by the French schoolteacher who seems to think we are setting a bad example to her students. Trying hard to follow the official footpath we soon notice that the pavement has ceased and we are walking on the motorway hard shoulder. A variety of greetings are exhibited to us by passing lorry drivers. Eventually after trudging through wild storms over the busy high Seine bridge Karen spots a beautiful barn converted into a comfortable gite! We are here in Du Milieu for the night now. 23 damp miles today. We'll try to break fewer laws tomorrow!

Thursday 15th - Friday 16th May

A beautiful day's walking today through the dense forest. Across the Seine again, this time by ferry, to a good campsite at Jumieges. We dine on pizza in a friendly local bar. Here we are considered the novelty customers of the day by the regulars who make it clear that their idea of a good walk is from home to the bar. This is the first night for my new lighter tent bought in Portsmouth and it seems to be ok. Friday 16th we go back across the Seine on a different ferry further up stream, then along the riverbank to another dense forest. We lose our direction in this one so the supposedly shorter day turns out to be much longer than planned! We also find that the advertised campsite does not exist in Elbeuf, so we have taken rooms in the economy class Hotel du Progres where the townspeople are gathered for Friday Bingo Night. My wet washing is draped around the room to dry.

Saturday 17th - Sunday 18th May

A very wet day's walking brings us to Acquiny and the family home of Amnesty supporters Annick, Jean and Giles Quere who welcome us into their overnight care with warm towels to dry ourselves, hot tea and Waitrose biscuits. Jean is the recently elected Deputy Mayor. We are advised that the local press are on their way to interview us and to my delight a teacher of English from the local school is already here to help with translation. After the formalities of the interviews and photographs we get our first real taste of French family hospitality at the dinner table where stimulating conversation is equally as important as good food. Annick and Jean arrange further accommodation for us in a few days time with friends of theirs before waving us off in the morning to another damp day's walk. We are now 99 miles into France, on day 18 of this interesting journey. Arriving in Pacy sur Eure somewhat wet and scruffy we take late lunch in a rather smart hotel where our style of dress is again the novelty of the day, this time for the elegant locals. Considering the inclement weather we negotiate a reasonably priced room here and are settled on the top floor of the annexe. No matter how much wet washing we spread around we fail to completely cover the orange striped wallpaper.

Pacy sur Eur	10 miles	Ivry-la-Bataille
Ivry-la-Bataille	→ 15 miles ←	Conde-sur-Vesgres
Conde-sur-Vesgres	15 miles	Rambouillet
Rambouillet	15 miles	St. Cheron

Monday 19th - Thursday 22nd May

Just a few light showers today as we make our way to Ivry-la-Bataille, a small town criss-crossed with rivers and streams. We eventually find the municipal campsite but it is mostly occupied by permanent caravan dwellers, one of whom asks us to leave and come back when the warden returns in three hours time. Karen, in her most polite French, explains that we actually don't have anywhere else to go for the three hours and we settle on an empty plot with our clothes hung on the fencing to dry. Finally we are granted permission by telephone, pay five Euros each, and the grass is cut for us to pitch the tents. On the 20th we reach the de la Mare aux Biches campsite near Conde-sur-Vesgres where they are more accustomed to overnight guests and sell us sausage and chips. The 21st and we've reached Rambouillet with its beautiful chateau and well appointed Huttopia campsite. Removing my right sock in the shower I find a strange red liquid is leaking from a burst blister on the sole of this foot. Unable to raise the others on the mobile 'phone I stagger/hop back to the tents where Karen dresses the wound. The 22nd is St. Cheron. Spotting us looking confused as we study the map a friendly local lady shows us the way across the town park and up a steep track to the next campsite.

St. Cheron	12 miles	Boissy-le-Cutte
Boissy-le-Cutte ⟶	15 miles ⟵	Milly-la-Foret
Milly-la-Foret	15½ miles	Veneux-les-Sablons

Friday 23rd - Sunday 25th May

This bright sunny day leads us to the village of Boissy-le-Cutte. We haven't planned to stay here, but an appetising and enjoyable lunch, followed by the advice that there are a couple of good campsites only half a mile away, tempts us. When we return to the bar in the evening we find our travelling appearance has prompted interest from the landlord, and a lady from elsewhere in the village is called in to ask us in English all the burning questions the others want answered. We are the novelty of the day again! An important footnote for today is to mention that of the two campsites on offer at this location, we choose the one where patrons generally keep their clothes on. The naturist one is in the woodland behind us, next door. Saturday's stroll brings us to Milly-la-Foret, a campsite almost overrun by twenty-something's who are here for the rock climbing popular in this region. Sunday we arrive at Veneux-les-Sablons where the campsite is just on the edge of town. Here we have the luxury of sharing a rented mobile home with Karen's sister Heather, her partner and their two lively young sons. Typical of small French towns on a Sunday, all the restaurants are closed in the evening, so we eat take-away frozen pizza bought from the campsite office.

Monday 26th - Tuesday 27th May

We all make our way to the beautiful ornate gardens of the chateau at Fontainebleau where the boys complete their own sponsored walk [in aid of our two charities] despite the pouring rain. We then warm ourselves up with hot drinks and ice cream in a cafe before Austin *drives* us to Vulaines-sur-Seine where we are greeted by Danielle and Serge Ceruti - the friends of Jean and Annick. We are again treated to homely French hospitality and more stimulating conversation over a splendid dinner. Tuesday 27th, after a substantial breakfast, Serge kindly *drives us back* to the point where we left off walking near Fontainebleau and we begin today's trudge in fairly heavy rain. Somewhat traffic-splashed we stop for a mid-morning break in a friendly bar, where the resident landlord Jean Jacques, supporting the theme of our pilgrimage, gives us sandwiches, dried fruit snacks for later and a 'Swiss army' style penknife each. We promise to say prayers for him and his wife on arrival in Rome. More rain, then a nice lunch in a small restaurant, prepared by an interesting chef. We then go on to seek the advertised campsite at

Villeneuve la Guyard only to discover that it has closed down. After much discussion and deliberation we end up camping at the rough end of a cul-de-sac, behind a rusty old car with no windows, doors, seats or engine! How the pampered are humbled. We are grateful for the fact that we manage to pitch the tents just before a raging thunderstorm bursts overhead. Counting my blessings of the day I find as I drift off to sleep I am also praying for drier weather tomorrow.

Wednesday 28th - Saturday 31 May

This night in Sens, at the municipal campsite. Damp again! Thursday 29th we are at le Bruleries, 35 miles on from Fontainebleau in a gite with a kitchen, so we are cooking for the first time since Hollybush in Herefordshire. Lots more rain overnight and this morning, but warmed up this afternoon. We manage to wash and dry a few clothes and get the tents and sleeping bags dry too. Slightly fairer weather anticipated in the next few days [hopefully]. We met some English people today, so more sponsorship gained. We are bit tired, at least Karen and I are, Andy seldom admits to such things. Friday 30th we are in St. Florentin. The campsite here is by the river, so we are serenaded to sleep by the melodious frogs. Saturday 31st we reach Tonnerre where the campsite is very close to the side of the Canal de Bourgogne - handy for the early morning start along the towpath.

Tonnerre	13 miles	Ancy le France
Ancy le France →	17 miles	← Montbard
Montbard	22 miles	Vitteaux
Vitteaux	17 miles	Pont de Pany

Sunday 1st - Wednesday 4th June

Steady trekking along the canal towpath, today as far as
Ancy le France where we stay in the Hotel du Centre and
enjoy a grand lunch. Monday 2nd we are back along the
towpath. A passing vessel, the Nancy May, shows British
colours and we engage the owners in conversation,
resulting in our bags being carried onboard for us for the
rest of the day. We enjoy tea onboard before waving
farewell and walking to the next campsite at Montbard.
Tuesday 3rd brings us to the old town of Vitteaux where a
lady, spotting our backpacks, stops her car in the street to
talk to us. We are advised that she is the person
responsible for the municipal campsite and, giving us
directions to it, she turns her car around to re-open the
office and book us in. This office is actually the disused
railway station, the campsite being created on the vacated
railway land. We are the only patrons tonight. Andy and
Karen erect their tent in true traveller style whereas I go
for the lazier option and simply roll out my sleeping mat and
bag on the floor of the very clean shower block. We feast
ourselves on takeaway pizza bought from a travelling van
that boasts a proper wood fired oven. These pizzas are
generously stacked with toppings and absolutely delicious.
Wednesday 4th we stroll on to Pont de Pany where we
meet my cousin John at our pre-arranged rendezvous
beside the bridge.

Thursday 5th - Sunday 8th June

We've been going along well despite the very variable weather and have now passed the 500 mile barrier, so very much enjoying our few days off. We are staying with my cousin John and his wife Lillian who live over here in Varennes throughout the 'summer'. The weather continues to be quite wet with mists restricting the best local views. We understand there's snow in the mountains ahead of us, so knowing there are more surprises in store we take great pleasure in, and full advantage of, John and Lilli's hospitality. On the morning of Sunday 8th John kindly drives us back to the exact spot by the canal bridge at Pont de Pany where we left off and we continue along the towpath to our next campsite at Dijon. After some mild confusion in the office we are allocated a plot next to a young English couple who become our latest generous sponsors. We take the bus into Dijon Central for a bit of sightseeing and dinner, but walk back to our site. Another wild and furious thunder and rain storm pounds the city, so we are forced to wait for quite a while under the wide railway bridge until it rumbles off into the distance.

Dijon	21 miles	St. Jean de Losne
St. Jean de Losne ⟶	14½ miles ⟵	Longwy
Longwy	22 miles	Arbois

Monday 9th - Wednesday 11th June

Our last day on the canal, which is very straight with good paths. Beautiful skies today. Starting to see the first sign of the hills ahead of us. Camping again now but beside the river for a change, at St. Jean de Losne. Tuesday 10th we arrive in Chaussin, 34 miles south east of Dijon, in time for lunch but find the chef has gone home. We walk what turns out to be another three miles away from our intended route to find the campsite at Longwy, which has no food! We are saved by a lovely, elderly French couple who drive Karen to the supermarket two miles back so we can eat after all! Lovely sunny day again, so we are also able to wash and dry our clothes. Wednesday 11th and we are in Arbois, home of Louis Pasteur (he who liked to bathe in milk up over his eyes), 22 miles on from yesterday. For the first time this trip I am out in front all day, as Andy's left leg is playing up. Fortunately it is better at the end of the day following Ibuprofen, homeopathy and TLC in roughly equal parts. We are now seeing the change in terrain as the hills become mountains. There is a mountain region feel to the countryside now as more of the houses we see are in the Swiss chalet style and the cattle and goats are now sporting sweetly tinkling bells around their necks.

Thursday 12th - Friday 14th June

Steadily rising through this beautifully changing rural landscape we come round a hillside road corner to see our day's destination, the old walled hilltop town of Nozeroy. [Altitude 789 metres]. Down into the valley we go, then back up the other side, keeping a watchful eye out for any sign of the advertised campsite. We finally locate the small site after much searching, but it is closed and the sign says 'Campervans Only'. Close examination of the toilet facilities sends us back into the centre of town where we are warmly welcomed at the small family run Hotel des Ramparts. The kitchen is closed, but we are allowed to use the dining room, so picnic on goodies hastily purchased from the local shop. Friday 13th, and our route from Nozeroy starts downhill, flattens out with clear views of the approaching mountains, then rises to 1000 metres through managed forests before falling again to reach Mouthe (pronounced Moot) where we expect, from symbols on the map, to find a campsite, but discover again that it's a couple of kilometres in the wrong direction. Checking out the alternatives whilst I sit in a cafe drinking hot chocolate, Karen books us into a gite where we are later joined by a large group of French walkers on the start of a weekend break. We are lulled to sleep by their enthusiastic cheering of a televised football match, right outside our door!

Saturday 14th June

Ahead of us as we leave Mouthe is a wall of forest rising
steadily again up the mountainside. We pass by the
unmanned French and Swiss border posts, which are really
just a couple of large wooden sheds about 100 metres
apart. The border posts are both closed, so we leave
France and enter Switzerland incognito with memories of Le
Havre creating a brief feeling of 'déjà vu'. We drop down
the Swiss side to the shores of Lac des Joux, then back up
again to our pre-booked night's accommodation in the eco
friendly Tipi Village near the mountain top. 1200 metres
above sea level here with a distinct chill in the air. These
tipi tents are just like the native American version with
a wood chip floor and a ring of stones for a fireplace. The
provided dinner consists of copious amounts of soup,
cheese and fresh local bread, washed down with beer, wine
or fruit juice. The other tipi's are occupied tonight by a
large group of family and friends celebrating one young
lady's birthday, so we get shares of the cake. Even lighting
the open fire in the tipi doesn't fully deter the chill in the air,
so I sleep with all my clothes still on and the hood of my
sweatshirt up. This certainly qualifies as the most unusual
place we have stayed since the church porch in Droxford.

Sunday 15th June

We rise and slip quietly away without disturbing the birthday revellers, head further up the mountain enjoying the splendid early morning views out across the lake, then make our way down the other side towards the shores of Lake Geneva. All my internal pride at achieving this mountain top is shattered by the lady who passes us near the top but going in the other direction. This trekker is overcoming the challenge of the mountain and her unsuitable legs by using double elbow crutches. Feeling suitably humbled, but full of the joy of life, I lead the way down the path. We lunch in a small town near the waterside which accepts our payment in Euros then make our way along the water's edge footpath, stopping at a cash machine to obtain as many Swiss Francs as we can in one transaction. A couple of hours of steady hiking along the shoreline establish us as the 'stare at novelty of the day' for the fashionable after-lunch strollers. Early evening we reach the well-appointed campsite at Lausanne where we are again serenaded to sleep by enthusiastic football supporters, [the joy of travelling at 'World Cup' time], this time mostly supporting the Netherlands.

Monday 16th - Wednesday 18th June

Monday's lakeside stroll brings us eventually to Montreux where we take rooms in a budget hotel. Comfort at a reasonable cost, but it is almost possible to touch the high speed trains that rattle past the bedroom window. Our three night stay here gives us free time to spend with Andy's brother Peter and sister-in-law Gill, who have flown here on holiday to meet up with us. Together we visit the magnificently preserved fairytale castle Chillon which inspired Lord Byron's famous, rather mournful poem, 'The Prisoner of Chillon'. A very pleasant day is spent crossing the lake by ferryboat and we sample a few of Montreux's mostly rather over-priced restaurants. Despite the expense this is an enjoyable little 'side holiday' with Peter and Gill, whose sponsorship again boosts the minibus fund. As we leave Montreux Peter kindly takes our tents from us to help reduce the weight on our backs. We are now on the official Pilgrimage route to Rome, so staying in Pilgrim accommodation as often as possible is now the plan.

Thursday 19th - Friday 20th June

Well, today we can consider ourselves proper pilgrims as we leave the expensive decadence of Montreux behind and make our way just over 17 miles further south east to the large and ancient abbey of St. Maurice, commenced year 515 and used continuously since. The Hospitalier Priest who sees us to our rooms and to our meal (omelette, salad and chips) tells us they get an average of two or three pilgrims a week through here, so we hope to meet more from now on as we haven't met any others yet! The wide space between the mountains occupied by Lake Geneva is now also behind us and we can see the width of the valley closing in around as we head gradually upwards toward the St. Bernard pass in a few days time. Warmer weather is here at last but is not promised to hold for long. We are not disheartened by this forecast though as the Priest says when there is snow the pilgrims simply ski over the pass! Friday 20th and a hearty breakfast in the Abbey sets us off for a further 20 miles of steadily rising pathwork to La Douay where we have pre-booked rooms at the Hotel Le Gite. As we check in the patron advises us that the restaurant next door is about to close, so we hastily remove our packs to dash in for dinner. Our dishevelled appearance causes less interest than usual, but we are still the novelty group to a few who stare interestedly.

35

Saturday 21st June

The path we are now following is generally quite clearly marked, though there are a few misleading signs and some stretches that 'look right', but lead to dead ends, forcing us to retrace our hill weary steps. Eventually we reach the town of Bourg-St-Pierre where we have pre-booked a room for three in hostel accommodation above an all pine decor restaurant. After laying out our sleeping bags and taking our turns in the shower we explore this picture postcard town, ending up sunbathing outside the municipal swimming pool before returning to sample the delights of the restaurant.

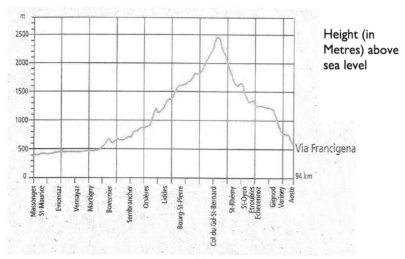

Sunday 22 June 2008

According to 'official' timings given in the guide leaflets this rising walking journey from Bourg-St-Pierre [1,632m] to the Hospice at the top of the St. Bernard Pass [2,469m] should take four hours. We take a more leisurely approach. Karen and Andy both bathe their feet in the cool mountain stream water along the way whilst I choose to keep my boots on and enjoy instead the role of photographer. 2469m – that's 7500ft – or, for our Herefordshire supporters, five times the height of Hay Bluff, and it does feel like it! I am so glad we are doing this whilst I am still young. Today there are three live snakes crossing our path and we fall over a good few times in the snow, but feel elated drinking the welcoming cups of hot fresh tea provided in the Hospice. Walking and cycling pilgrims, and other cross-country mountaineers, are allowed to stay in the Pilgrim Hospice du Grand St. Bernard which has been here on this site for more than 1000 years. I am pleased to discover that the mattresses are new this century. After visiting the remaining descendants of the famous St. Bernard dogs and viewing the museum, we spend a very pleasant evening in the company of Nicolas and Muriel, a friendly young Swiss couple also staying at the Hospice, who are crossing our path at this famous point while trekking the mountain tops east to west.

Meetings and conversations such as these are the life blood of pilgrimage.

Nicholas and Muriel write:

"Here are a few pictures from three Brits we met last Sunday at the hospice du Grand St. Bernard, which is located at the border between Switzerland and Italy. It's one of the easily accessible paths across the Alps. People walking from north to south have been stopping by the priests for almost 1000 years now. You can get good food, comfortable beds and warmth.

"Oh Rome-eo, wherefore art thou?"
"About 500 miles up the road-eo Pete!"

The Grand St. Bernard really is a majestic place! While Karen, Andy and Peter saw several snakes along the path (apparently Peter hates snakes!), they kept their smiles and happiness. This warmed the cold and thin air and gave the Hospice a little home sweet home feeling. Thanks a lot for the good time we spent together. Good luck along the Italian roads and enjoy the pasta and the gelati!"

Nicolas and Muriel

Nicolas and Muriel tell us "This is the way up…"

"… and this is
the way
down!"

Peter, Karen and Andy feeling on top of he world - well, almost

Monday 23rd - Wednesday 25th June

After breakfast we are treated to a private blessing in the Hospice church before crossing the Swiss/Italian border and starting the 6000 feet steep downhill trek to the modern Roman city of Aosta, where we take a day's rest in the Hotel Belle Epoque, pilgrim-priced and right in the centre of town. We are now in the land of the greatest selection of ice creams available, so I have started testing them all, in the name of scientific research of course! We feel entitled to this break as we are now 740 miles from Logaston or 750 miles from Clifford. Andy calculates this as well over half way on every version of the map. Our second evening finds us enjoying a special pilgrim menu in an old Roman basement, which was probably on street level when constructed. On the 25th we head almost due east along the Aosta valley, mostly following the path which is some way up on the northern mountainside, giving panoramic views over the bustling industry below. Nineteen miles on from Aosta tonight we are in another small hotel offering special rates for pilgrims, this one, the Hotel Dufour in Chatillon, is on a busy street corner. Here the traffic noise competes with the local brass band practising all evening in the next building. We know this is definitely Italy when the sound of the band is finally replaced by the frequent honking of scooter horns.

Thursday 26th - Saturday 28th June

Continuing almost due east along the Aosta valley as that's the only way out of these mountains, tonight we are in Pont St Martin and La Grange, an agriturismo small flat next to a working farm. The morning of the 27th we leave the Alps behind and turn back to our south-east direction again. We have booked a room in advance at the newly built large convent in Ivrea, but decline on arrival as the cost is much higher than

expected, finding instead a comfortable affordable Ikea furnished apartment. Saturday 28th our route along small country lanes and byways brings us to Santhia overnight. The Hotel - Ristorante Vittoria, opposite the railway station, is recommended to us by friendly local people. Their advice is good. We find this establishment is also patronised by a sizeable group of people with learning difficulties and their accompanying parents, with whom we share the good varied buffet supper and breakfast. The weather is now boiling us so we are getting up very early, 5.30am, to be able to cover 6 to 7 miles before it gets too hot. Today I drank 1½ litres of milk, a litre of orange juice, half a litre of lemonade and about the same of water and still arrived thirsty! People at the road side have stopped asking where we are going as they now generally presume it is Rome. Second language here is still French, so they are wishing us 'bon voyage'. No problems drying the washing in this heat, it dries in moments.

Sunday 29th June - Monday 30th

Two days of endless rice and maize fields full of mosquitoes. Sunday's hosts are the monks of the Convento di Billiemme in Vercelli. Whilst we are out in the town eating pizza a rainstorm suddenly appears, but we return to find they have thoughtfully taken in our washing. A comfortable night then another early start. This route through Italy is so poorly marked and rarely walked that, as has been the case before when following the signs, we are stranded mid-field at a dead end, miles from anywhere with our only options being trying to retrace our steps a couple of miles or go along the railway line. We take the railway option for about another mile until it meets a road, then walk into Mortara town looking as innocent as possible! We stay on Monday in Sant Albino, an old monastery being modernised with Ferrari money to a decent standard. We share with two other pilgrims - the first we have met so far, a young English couple going from Rome to Canterbury on foot, mostly for fun but also for World Wildlife Fund. We have lots to talk about and it is useful to swap tips on how to ward off the various snakes we have all encountered. It seems we have more vipers ahead as well as behind us!

Tuesday 1st - Wednesday 2nd July

Today's walk past more fields of rice and maize brings us to an unusual sort of building in woodland on the outskirts of the town of Zerbolo. The Cascina Venara feels like some sort of youth camp by the layout and furnishings but has clearly not been used for some time as there is thick dust in my dormitory. It is very nice to see storks nesting on poles at the end of the garden, but a bit disconcerting to find a large stuffed one upside down occupying the bunk opposite mine! I just have to hope that the taxidermist does not return in the middle of the night! Should make for some disturbing dreams.......

After our night in the rarely-cleaned semi-closed hostel, we make our mosquito ridden way to the big city of Pavia. We are staying two nights here in a beautiful big room with its own kitchenette and spacious bathroom, provided to us pilgrims by the Caritas Diocesana of Pavia, which seems to be the social service of this diocese. We are not obliged to pay but donations are welcomed. This is an interesting vibrant city with lots of old churches dotted among the modern shops. Making the most of our time we get a lot of essential jobs done. Andy's irritating tooth is filled, my backpack re-stitched, Karen and I have our hair cut [separate establishments] and a few heavier items are sent home by post. As a sideline we also manage some sightseeing.

<u>Friday 4th - Monday 7th July</u>

Marginally fewer mosquitoes harass us on the paths and byways to Santa Cristina where we stop for the night in the parochial sports centre. Here there are dozens of children playing, painting pictures, doing organised sports and singing. The people are again very welcoming, giving us free iced drinks on arrival and showing us our rooms. We are trustingly and generously given free run of everywhere for the night. At the suggestion of making a donation the resident Priest declines with a wave of his hand, saying the Parish takes care of everything. The radiant smiles and laughter of the many children are testimony to the truth of his statement. The 5th of July is still very hot, but thankfully with fewer mosquitoes as we ramble on to Orio Litta. Arriving in town and searching for the address of the pre-booked pilgrim accommodation our eyes settle on a sort of 'medieval' looking horseshoe shaped building in old red brick. We stop for a drink and rest, then photograph this unusual attractive piece of architecture, before continuing our search. We pass a bar, map in hand, checking street numbers. The community here clearly prides itself on its helpfulness as almost all the customers of the bar leap up to

call our attention and one goes off to find the man we are
seeking. We are greeted, then taken back to the building
we'd been admiring as the rooms allocated to us are in its
tower. Later, back in the bar, we read in the local paper
that this tastefully refurbished building has been in use as a
pilgrim hostel for the last ten years and the first book of
records has just been completed, so our entry will be the
first page in the next handsome leather bound volume -
quite an honour. Attached to this first page will be our
sponsorship form and map. Here we meet and share
rooms with our first Italian pilgrim, a young man from
Naples walking on his own from Rome to Canterbury. This
meeting affords us the opportunity for cultural exchange
and the chance for both parties to learn some of the pitfalls
of the routes ahead. The 6th of July we are in Piacenza,
small city with a very ornate fronted cathedral. The 7th in
the church dormitory of Fiorenzuola, another small town
that seems to be largely closed on Mondays. Close now to
the end of the flatlands, we can see the hills looming ahead.
The endless rice fields with their teams of pilgrim eating
mosquitoes will not be missed!

Well over the 900 mile mark now and looking forward to
breaking the 1000 mile barrier in the hill country ahead.
Still crazily hot in the mid-day and afternoons, so we are

rigidly sticking to
our 5.30am alarm
and start walking
as soon as
possible
afterwards.

Just beginning to
see fields of
tomatoes now,
they make a
pleasant change.

Tuesday 8th - Wednesday 9th July

A short (11 mile) walk today on easy roads and tracks has brought us to Fidenza (a larger city than we had expected) and into the care of the Franciscan monastery/church, the Convento S. Francesco, where we are settled for the night. We are very well fed and cared for by the monks and others here with a substantial dinner and breakfast at no charge, which greatly helps our rapidly reducing personal bank balances. Bidding farewell to this happy monastic community we start to climb the path through the hills as our route takes its turn towards the coast. Our later start after breakfast with the monks makes us very grateful for the shade as we walk. Our trudging through miles of rice fields, pursued by flying things determined to eat us at every opportunity is now behind us, as we have entered the hill country and escaped them and some of the humidity that goes with large scale irrigation. We are told though that there are more ahead yet! Oh to be a pilgrim! Our spirits brightened today by the beautiful, undulating countryside and by the large family along the way who called us into their home. They gave us lasagne, our first in Italy, then sponsored us as well. Thanks Jamie, Valerie and family.

Such kindness and generosity lifts the heart. Tonight we are again in a small pilgrim friendly hotel, the Picchio Rosso, in Medesano. Reasonably priced, with a buffet in the restaurant below.

Thursday 10th - Saturday 12th July

Our hill path and country road ramblings today bring us to Sivizzano, a tiny town in a valley where we are accommodated in the parish hall. This is a medieval barrel-vaulted, ancient remnant of an earlier monastery long since lost to history. The friendly parishioners were busy preparing the room for a wedding but one helped us a lot by taking us to a supermarket, and the kindly priest showed us how to make beds using two wooden pews facing each other with a mattress on top or laying unopened trestle tables face up on the floor. Now partly below ground due to centuries of change, the room was pleasant and with an even, cool temperature. We move on early the next morning (11th) across streams and over hill paths to Berceto, where the young priest meets us in the centre of town and takes us to a large residential school, the Ostello del Seminario, where 150 children are having great fun playing outside. I guess it's the end of term party as the staff are busy baking them cakes. We are asleep long before the children. Saturday 12th's walk starts with a steady climb through woodland to around 1000 metres to a peak with fantastic views over this range, before descending to the ancient town of Pontremoli where the Franciscan monastery, another Convento S. Francesco, is our lodging place for tonight. It is still very hot and sunny here every day with temperatures reaching the 30s by lunchtime most days. This brings out the most beautiful butterflies in great numbers to add to the pleasure of the scene.

Sunday 13th July 2008

Another longish day with
mostly ups and downs again
through forests and hillside
villages. Some rain off and on,
so we are putting on and removing waterproofs for a while.
Highlights of today are passing the 1000 mile point,
achieving halfway through our trek in Italy, meeting an old
man who praises us as pilgrims for breaking down barriers
between the different people of the world, and the
unknown lady who stops her car, jumps out to run over to
us to say 'hello' then hands me a carrier bag before driving
off again. The bag contains about a kilo of watermelon, half
a kilo of ice cream and a loaf of still warm bread. I barely
have time to wave thanks as she speeds away. Such moving
generosity. We enjoy these gifts at tonight's lodging, the
Chiesa di San Carpasio, in Aulla.

Monday 14th July

To reach Sarzana we hike ten miles today under rumbling
clouds, over hills with medieval villages perched on them
just like picture postcards. At one point we have to dive
for cover into a farm building as the heavens open with such
gusto that the paths run like rivers. In the sunshine that
follows we are treated to beautiful views of the sea we will
reach tomorrow. We are in a mushroom growing area, so I
order the mushroom ice cream, just to see what it is like to
taste. It is actually, by Italian standards, a fairly basic
coloured vanilla, moulded into the mushroom shape.
Although mildly disappointed, I eat it all the same.

Tuesday 15th July

Day 76 since I left Clifford and only 21days to Rome if all goes well and according to plan! Today we arrive at the seaside, Massa Marina to be precise. This is our one 'touch' at the sea this trip (apart from the English Channel). It seems strange to be amongst all these people taking their summer holidays in their best beach fashions as we plod along between them with our big boots and backpacks, wearing the same travel beaten clothes we have worn for the last two and a half months. The vast majority of the seafront here is privatised, with gaudy cafes and restaurants blocking views of the sea to anyone with an empty wallet who is less than ten feet tall. Not even in the top fifty for enjoyable stops on this route, but we strip off our outer layers to lie on the small public beach with the best of the poor people. We rest the night at the Cambini rooms, a slightly bohemian, very clean and friendly guest house a few hundred metres back from the seafront.

<u>Wednesday 16th July</u>

Today we curve back inland to go through the 4/5ths of the journey stage as we head for Lucca in two days time. Back to beautiful sunshine in cloudless skies and we spend this night a little further inland, in Camaiore at the Hotel Le Monache, another lovely little hotel, as this region is a little short on parochial dwellings. Some quiet and pleasant paths in the hills again but some wild traffic on roads without pavements also. This is the marble quarrying region of Italy, so we have passed many mason's yards with enormous blocks of white or coloured marble being cut by large, water cooled mechanical saws, into sheets about an inch thick.

Thursday 17th - Saturday 19th July

Tonight we are in Lucca, a lovely old walled city, reached from our last town on a mix of roads and paths. We met our first other pilgrims going the same way and just like the buses, three came along at once! 19th July finds us in Altopasciao in more parochial rooms, this time in a modern building alongside the sports facilities above what appears to be the young people's job and gap year opportunity centre. Some strange internal construction flaws make me think this building was designed by a committee who didn't ever quite agree. There's a lovely 'wet room' style shower in the ground floor toilet for people with disabilities, but no drain in the floor, just a mop and bucket. The first floor shower is of the 'spray anywhere and everywhere' variety with nowhere to keep one's clothes dry, so it is necessary to dash naked into the mixed sex passageway outside to get dried and dressed!

Sunday 20th July

Off the flat and starting to rise again. Quite a lot of road today but as it is Sunday, very little traffic. Part of the route is on a 10th century Roman road, still in excellent condition. One long snake sends shivers down my spine today when I spot it slithering a little too close to the path for my comfort. Tonight we are in San Miniato Basso, where the pilgrim accommodation is in the Misericordia, which in Britain would translate to a combined cottage hospital, ambulance and fire station, with its own chapel. The people are very welcoming, presenting us with gilt certificates of our progress. The thought strikes me that I have at last been certified and hospitalised at the same time. Many have suggested this as an appropriate course of action in the past. Karen and Andy have the pilgrim room and I settle down in the modern chapel alongside.

Monday 21st July

A long dry hot walk today up and down a number of hills.
Beautiful views over the rolling countryside and lots of sad
looking, abandoned, large old farm houses. Tonight we are
in the parish hall in Gambassi, on the top of the last of
today's hills. Constructed in the 1950s in the 'small theatre/
community cinema' style, the room has no beds or shower
facilities and has clearly seen better days. We are, however,
warmly welcomed by the priest and a night sleeping on the
stage will be another of the adventures of this journey. One
dead snake on the road today.

Tuesday 22nd July

Tuesday finds us in San Gimignano (pronounced jiminyarno), another hill top town where the striking tall medieval towers and well preserved basillica (cathedral) are a magnet for many tourists. The choice of this town for the film set of 'Tea with Mussolini' has also helped. The ice cream shop (gelateria) patronised by Tony Blair is also busy! We are in a Convent tonight, separate rooms with own bathrooms, so a step up in comfort from nine miles back. About five miles back, a very nice man named Mario called out to us as we passed his house inviting us in for tea or coffee and biscuits. He had spoken in English as he had been expecting us, from the advice of the Italian pilgrims we have been shadowing these last few days. We expect to see them somewhere on the way tomorrow to thank them.

Wednesday 23rd July

Monteriggioni. This fortress town looks from a distance like it could have been designed by a ten year old boy using empty cereal boxes as it has evenly spaced square towers, separated by long straight lengths of wall. It sits neatly on the top of the hill, so is an imposing sight. We are accommodated in a friendly and welcoming pilgrim hostel next to the church in the central square. This night promises to be the best so far as we will be enjoying a meal with at least three other pilgrims. Our two new friends from Milan and Anna who welcomed us to our lodgings. She is herself an accomplished pilgrim, being the famed person we first heard of way back in St. Maurice. Anna is the lone lady who left Canterbury in December 2007, crossing the Grand St. Bernard alone in the middle of winter on borrowed snow shoes. An interesting evening spent swapping travellers' tales before we sleep, ready to tackle the short stroll into Siena in the morning.

Thursday 24th July

We leave Monteriggioni early to get ahead of the heat but
are quickly caught up by Anna, who is heading out to make
watercolour sketches in the early morning light. We
gratefully accept the gift of two from her portfolio before
waving farewell. Arriving in Siena today about 12 midday to
be welcomed by the Sisters of Charity of San Vincenzo who
are our hosts for our two night stay here. A well known
city of the renaissance, we visit the ornate marble cathedral
and a couple of ice cream shops. The evening meal is a
buffet of pizza of every variety, prepared by the young
volunteers who help the three nuns operate this sizeable
social facility. One of the team, a fashionable petite young
lady, is celebrating her birthday and her friends jokingly
taunt her with the suggestion that she should celebrate
properly by joining us for the rest of the way to Rome. She
looks at us and politely declines.

Friday 25th July

Our day off here in Siena is very rewarding. We visit a further selection of churches, then go to see the 15th century pilgrim hospital, only closed last century, which is interesting and we are able to count our blessings of the 21st century comforts and hospitality the Sisters are providing for us. Below the hospital are the lengthy, intriguing catacombs that now house the museum of Roman and earlier relics. We seem to go down and down forever before emerging much further down the hill on the other side. Tonight there are Tyrolean, Bulgarian, Romanian, Orcadian, Italian, Indian, Australian and English pilgrims together, so conversations have been most educational, especially for me, as my only two languages are English and rubbish.

Saturday 26th July

My mobile 'phone alarm calls out 'It is time to get up, the time is 5.30' and there is an immediate rugby scrum for the bathroom as eight people attempt to reach one of the two loos. I myself had found a staff loo on the ground floor last night, so avoided the rush. We enjoy our yoghurt, milk and frizzante (fizzy water) in the entrance hall, then get away to an early start. Tonight in Ponte D'Arbia (bridge over the Arbia). A very small but welcoming community with pilgrim beds in a room at the side of the parish hall. On the 'phone we were advised where to find the key, then two local teenage lads arrived to show us how to manage and leave the facility. A children's party is in full swing for the afternoon/evening, so we shall have a juvenile chorus to lull us to sleep. The shop was shut when we arrived, but the bar opens at six in the morning for breakfast.

Sunday 27th July

Ponte D'Arbia to San Quirico is a pleasant, short Sunday morning stroll. We sit on the steps of one of the three churches and are met by a curly haired, curly bearded, young man in Bermuda shorts and Hawaiian shirt who shows us to the pilgrim room in the back of the church, leaving us to shower and wash our clothes with a message that he would attend to the paperwork after mass at 6.00am. I dutifully attend the mass to find that he is actually the priest. It is an enjoyable service, mostly in Italian but with one of the readings in English as well and ends with the usual congregational peace greeting, "pace" in Latin/Italian.

Monday 28th July

We are able to see our destination for today in the distance, on the far range of hills. We reach Radicofani after a long walk (18 miles) of good paths and roads. The only dark moment being when three of the white Roman cross sheepdogs, native to the area, decide to be aggressive and are, unfortunately, loose on the path so round for an attack. They let Andy and Karen pass with only a growl but see me as a lone target. Fortunately, I am only fearful of snakes, so telling them in my politest English that I have nothing for them whilst continuing walking allows me to escape! Our fellow pilgrims in tonight's hostel have a similar encounter later in the day. Tonight's hostel is run by the fraternity of St. James. We have been treated to a splendid vegetarian meal and had our feet ceremonially washed as a token of recognition of pilgrimage. Every day here is certainly full of different new experiences.

Tuesday 29th July

Waved off after an early breakfast by Marco and Louisa, we leave Radicofani, to head on to Acquapendente. En route today we cross the southern border of Tuscany to enter Lazio, the region that includes Rome as we are now just 90 miles from our destination. This is a big(ish) old walled town, as so many are on this ancient road. We are in an interesting building created out of the staircase for the bell tower of one church and the side wall of another. They must once have had very large congregations to warrant two churches so close together. It is a coal fired cooker so we are eating out tonight.

Wednesday 30th July

Very hot today and the path is largely on white gravel roads that both reflect the heat and cover us in dust when vehicles pass, but we are able to wash all that away here with the Sisters of San Sacramento in their convent in the centre of Bolsena town. This town has the same name as the sizeable lake it is built alongside. A short walk tomorrow, but heat expected again so we still need to be up before 5.30am.

Thursday 31st July

The route to Montefiascone is a short walk, only 9 miles, so one of our shortest days, however fiasco does mean fun. Unfortunately the clear signage we have been used to in recent times, goes a bit haywire today. At one stage, after the signs send us down a path to a wide stream we cannot cross, we rejoin the track to meet head on a troop of about a dozen scouts who are also heading to Montefiascone, but walking in the opposite direction! We leave them studying their map, then at the end of one of our short breaks beside the pilgrim oak at a crossroads, they re-appear and after some enjoyable chat they decide to follow the English. We are in a convent and they are camping, so we don't expect to see them again.

Friday 1st August

Our route today passes the volcanic hot springs, where we
join a few others bathing in the warm sulphurous waters.
An enjoyable side experience. We enter Viterbo through a
rambling array of suburbs, with what seems like Italy's
largest graveyard, concealing an intriguing old town with a
labyrinth pilgrim quarter. Here we finally find somewhere
to stay in the parochial accommodation of San Andrea.
Whilst sitting under a tree in town we are hailed by a
Spanish lady asking: "Are you the three famous English
pilgrims?" She had read many of our entries in the log
books in hostels along the way and had met the Australians!
A G.P. by 'trade' she recognised us by our feet! (which
because they are usually hidden in boots, are a startling
white compared to our brown legs). Soon afterwards, the
Italian couple that we had said farewell to a few days earlier
reappear to make us six at the table. Evening meal at the
paradise gardens rounds the day off nicely.

Saturday 2nd - Sunday 3rd August

Tonight we reach Sutri, a small ancient walled town where our hosts are the closed order of nuns of the Monache Carmelitane. We conduct procedures through a darkened grille, so we are unable to see the Sister on the other side. Payment and passports go into the rotating vertical half-barrel, one turn and back come the stamped passports and keys. After enjoying the pre-laid breakfast, where we can hear the melodic singing of the nuns but cannot see them, we place the keys in the appointed place and quietly leave. Sunday 3rd August we are en route for Campagnano when the mobile 'phone rings for a pre-arranged live interview on BBC Radio Hereford and Worcester. This type of thing is no doubt commonplace for international journalists, but a little unusual for a rambler like myself, but, with Andy and Karen's prompting and support I muddle my way through and the interviewer seems happy with the result! In Campagnano we are staying in rooms above the parochial hall. During the evening the priest appears with a selection of pizzas and drinks as a very welcome gift from his parish. We share tonight again with our Spanish friend.

Monday 4th August

The traffic and noise levels are an indication we are nearing the eternal city as we find our way to the Convent St. Brigida at La Storta. The accommodation here is quite luxurious, but also comparatively expensive. Maybe we've been 'spoilt' too often in the recent past! One of the nuns here has worked in Slough, quite near my west London home, and knows some of my friends with learning difficulties in Hillingdon. I am reminded that in some ways this is indeed a small world!

Tuesday 5th August

Our last day, just over ten miles, was never expected to hold any great surprises and it started just as expected. Like most large cities around the world, entry into Rome by foot requires a slog along busy dusty roads full of smelly bins and noisy traffic. We eventually came to a point where rounding a corner by a park afforded us a view of the city from one of the seven hilltops. At the base of this hill is the Olympic Village, now looking a little tired, where one of the larger marble faced buildings is now the Youth Hostel where we had pre-booked 'a room'. However we found that they had very strict rules on almost everything, including room sharing, so Andy and I would be in the men's dormitory on one floor, and Karen in the women's on a different floor. This surprised us after travelling through the country staying in so many Monasteries and Convents without any questions asked. Like any good journalist would say, we made our excuses and left! In town near the railway station we found a basic hotel, The Pellicioni, with a private bathroom for only a couple of Euros more. No surprise then that the Youth Hostel has in excess of a hundred vacancies at the height of the season!

Into the Vatican City for the end of journey photos, kindly taken by the French family sitting near the obelisk, then off to the Pilgrim Registration Office to claim our final stamps and be awarded our certificates of completion. This done we are now scrubbed and shaved (not Karen!) and can begin to blend in with the hundreds of other tourists.

August 5th is the day when it is traditionally supposed to snow on a particular church here, so we have supper with Monica, our Spanish pilgrim friend, then take our places in front of the church to await the event. The police brass band plays for ages in a rather static though well lit display, but they have still not switched on the snow machines an hour later and our feet are tired, so we go home to bed. A text message from Monica the next morning confirmed that the snow did eventually come, but she had watched it from a bar across the street! We have the rest of the week to enjoy the many sights.

FRATERNITA DI MISERICORDIA
DI
SAN MINIATO BASSO

Il Governatore di questa Fraternita

attesta che

Shackleton Peter Douglas

ha sostato presso questa Associazione sita sulla

Via Francigena

San Miniato Basso, li   20 Luglio 2008

Il Governatore

Franco Giorgi

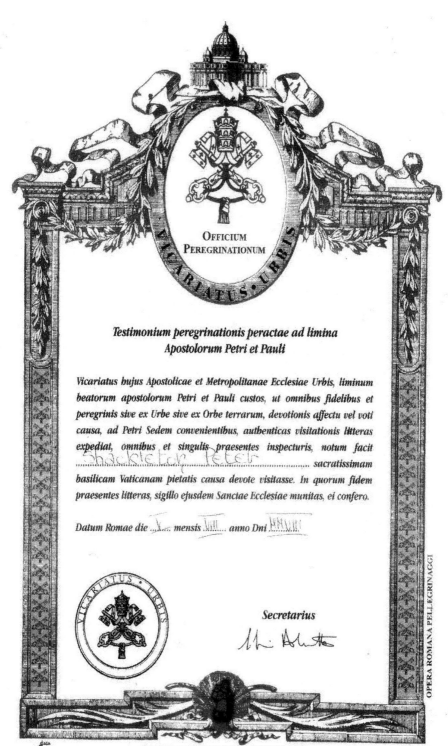

OFFICIUM
PEREGRINATIONUM

Testimonium peregrinationis peractae ad limina
Apostolorum Petri et Pauli

Vicariatus hujus Apostolicae et Metropolitanae Ecclesiae Urbis, liminum beatorum apostolorum Petri et Pauli custos, ut omnibus fidelibus et peregrinis sive ex Urbe sive ex Orbe terrarum, devotionis affectu vel voti causa, ad Petri Sedem convenientibus, authenticas visitationis litteras expediat, omnibus et singulis praesentes inspecturis, notum facit Shackleton Peter .... *sacratissimam basilicam Vaticanam pietatis causa devote visitasse. In quorum fidem praesentes litteras, sigillo ejusdem Sanctae Ecclesiae munitas, ei confero.*

Datum Romae die ... mensis ... anno Dni ...

Secretarius

OPERA ROMANA PELLEGRINAGGI

Conclusion

This book has been largely based on the notes I sent home to Hereford in the form of text messages from my mobile 'phone. These were then converted by Sarala and Jim into a 'blog' on the St. Owens website [www.fasoc.co.uk] as an easy means of keeping in contact with our supporters. The final entry on the blog contained part of what you've just read for Tuesday 5th August, followed by:

"We will fly home by Easyjet on Sunday.
For those who have enjoyed this blog - thanks for sticking with us
- on return I will be converting ... into a book which will be
available through this site with further profits to the St. Owens
Bus fund. - Minibuses need fuel -maintenance - dents knocked
out - and all the expenses we have with our private cars,
multiplied by the number of different drivers. Your sponsorship
support has been, and will continue to be, very greatly
appreciated. Now does anyone fancy a short walk to Sydney, or
maybe Tipperary or Timbuktu? - - - - - I am open to
suggestions...................."

We did, as planned, fly home by Easyjet on Sunday 10th August. The flight went smoothly and without incident until we were beginning the decent for Bristol. At this point the Chief Stewardess told the captive audience of passengers how the three of us had arrived in Rome on foot and something about our chosen charities. (She'd had an email from Matti's dad, an Easyjet pilot). We were asked to identify ourselves with a wave and were rewarded with a round of applause. In the terminal building queues for passport control and luggage our causes were treated to more very generous support from our fellow passengers. Karen's dad and sister then drove us back to Hereford, completing the final loop of this wonderful journey. At the date of publication no one has yet come forward seeking my companionship on the roads to Sydney, Tipperary or Timbuktu, but I remain cheerfully optimistic and, as always, open to suggestions.

Pilgrimage

The act of pilgrimage - travelling to places of particular religious or personal significance - has been practised in many cultures, and most religions at least as far back as the start of recorded history, and probably even before then. In this early part of the twenty first century the most popular and well known destinations include Lourdes, Canterbury, Santiago, Mecca, and of course Rome. All pilgrims have their own very personal reasons for such journeys. For me, as a fascinated student of life, the reasons are both complex and simple at the same time. The complexity comes from using the time spent walking for thinking about my life so far, my actions and reactions to circumstances I've been faced with, my family and friends and making plans for the future. The simplicity is in the basic joy of life on this planet. The beauty of the countryside, its wildlife, flora and fauna and the diversity, generosity and goodness of its people.

To my mind the best pilgrims are not necessarily those who travel the greatest distances, but those who build into their lives smaller, almost everyday journeys to help others. The neighbour who does the shopping for someone ailing or elderly, the parent who takes other children to school as well as their own, the volunteer who drives the minibus and the person who picks up something a stranger has dropped then hurries after them to give it back. Their journeys are as valuable and important as any thousand mile trek. They are the very fabric of civilised life. They are true twenty first century pilgrims.

About the authors

Peter Shackleton was born in Hillingdon, west London, in 1948. The youngest of the three children of Douglas and Edith Shackleton. Peter's sister Patricia led a life severely restricted by autism, his brother Robert was, from an early age, clearly the academic of the family, Peter was always the 'out and about' child.

Shortly after leaving school at 15 Peter was approached by the Uxbridge and District Society for Mentally Handicapped Children to see if he would become the leader of their proposed new Youth Club for mentally handicapped young people. Peter accepted this role, running the club for the following eight years and has been consistently involved with what has now become Mencap Hillingdon South and the Moorcroft Gateway Clubs ever since. After an 18 year career in photo lithography Peter transferred to residential care for people with learning disabilities in the early 1980s, qualifying as a social worker in 1986. He now works mostly in day care for people with learning disabilities, when he's not travelling!

Heather Russell was also born in Hillingdon, and met Peter some 30+ years ago when, at the age of 14, and as a member of 11th Hayes Girl Guides, she was introduced to Moorcroft Social Centre (Mencap Hillingdon South) in order to gain the 'Service Flash' badge. This entailed carrying out 40 hours of service in the community over 12 months. She has been involved with the group ever since and, needless to say, she got the badge! Heather now helps to run a weekly social club for people with learning disabilities, and organises two annual holidays for the group, as well as carrying on with her full-time day job as an Administrator, and studying part-time towards a degree in Literature and The Humanities with the Open University.

The St. Owens Centre, Hereford

The St. Owens Centre, opened in 1986 in the former boys' school, is situated in Symonds Street, close to the heart of Hereford city. The excellent service provided for adults with a wide range of learning and multiple disabilities is staffed and operated by the Social Services department of Herefordshire Council. Apart from sessions within the centre, students also attend further education courses through local colleges; work placements such as charity shops and the 'Community Cafe'; riding; recycling; and many other community based activities.

The Friends and Supporters of St. Owens Centre (*www.fasoc.co.uk*) is an independent charity which exists to provide support, both financial and caring, for the students at the centre. The Friends and Supporters own, in partnership with the Social Services department, one of the minibuses essential for the effective operation of the centre. At the time of going to press this bus is nearing the end of its useful life and the replacement fund is the beneficiary of the sponsors of Peter Shackleton on the Roam to Rome, and the sales of this book by the centre's Friends and Supporters.

Amnesty International

Amnesty International is a movement of ordinary people from across the world standing up for humanity and human rights. Their purpose is to protect individuals where justice, fairness, freedom and truth are denied. They are totally independent of government and are free to point out abuses of power regardless of religion or political standpoint. The Hereford, Leominster and Ludlow group is the collecting agent for the sponsors of Andy Johnson and Karen Stout on the Roam to Rome, and the sales of this book by their families, friends and supporters.

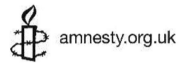 amnesty.org.uk

Mencap Hillingdon South, Moorcroft Gateway Clubs

What is now Mencap Hillingdon South started life in the early 1950s as a small group of parents and families of children with learning and multiple disabilities.

When the group began there were no special schools, day or residential centres in the area, so the parents themselves provided what they could for each other. A daytime group was established in a church hall, and

respite care was organised by those who had the room in their own homes and the energy and determination to cope. 'Professional' respite and long term care was only available in gigantic 'sub-normality' hospitals away in the countryside, and was very much a last resort.

The group's campaigning role, along with national pressure for change, has contributed greatly to what professional support there is available today. The Hillingdon North and South Mencap groups also built, own and run the hydrotherapy and swimming pool on the Moorcroft site, providing a very warm environment to those who cannot benefit from the much cooler public baths. This facility brings the wider Hillingdon community together as many other specialist support groups benefit from use of the pool, and many very small children learn to swim there too.

The Gateway Club met for the first time in May 1963 and now boasts three very diverse groups meeting regularly in the Social Centre at Moorcroft.

This Social Centre was the beneficiary of the 2004 pilgrimage to Santiago and is also benefiting from sales of this book in and around the Hillingdon community.

The sponsor form

Herefordshire to Rome Sponsored Walk

for Amnesty International & The St Owens Centre (Hereford)

In May 2008 Peter Shackleton and Andy Johnson will be setting off on an estimated 1,200 mile walk from north Herefordshire to Rome. Peter will be raising money for the St. Owens Centre in Hereford, Andy for Amnesty International.

We have some idea of what we're facing, having joined company for a slightly longer walk to Santiago de Compostela in north-west Spain in 2004, so all being well ....

If you would like to sponsor either of us, please complete the details on the next page of this form. We are suggesting that a total sum is specified, which can be paid on completion of the walk, or pro rata on the proportion of miles walked in the event of bodily breakdown en route! (Or you can pay in advance if feeling particularly generous and confident in our capacity.)

Brief details of each charity are given on the back page, and about us (below) for those of you who have been approached through an intermediary.

The outline route we will be following is shown on the map overleaf — which you can tear off and keep if you wish.

Please sponsor either or both of us for our two very deserving causes.
Many thanks.

Andy Johnson is known to his friends as someone who walks everywhere, so is adequately certified as being able at least to attempt this particular hike. His main work at present is running Logaston Press, a publisher of regional history, archaeology and guides, but he also chairs Kemble Housing Association, which provides affordable housing in Herefordshire.

A confirmed long distance trekker after tackling London to Santiago in 2004 **Peter Shackleton** is celebrating his 60th year in style with this journey. He says:-
'Walks like this are the best way to enjoy the countryside, and wherever you are going and travelling with Andy it is always a challenging adventure. Although I'm often some distance behind as I stop to look at the view, catch my breath and sniff the flowers, I know I can rely on my trusted guide to wait for me somewhere near the crossroads. Someday I may even get ahead (if I get up early enough, or don't go to bed)!

Peter Shackleton (above) on the road (literally) in France and Andy Johnson (below) in Logroño in Spain, having completed a day's walking, on our walk to Santiago de Compostela in 2004

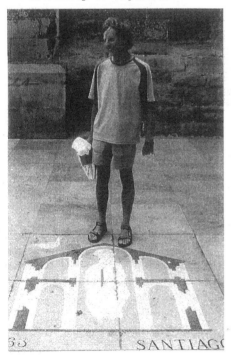

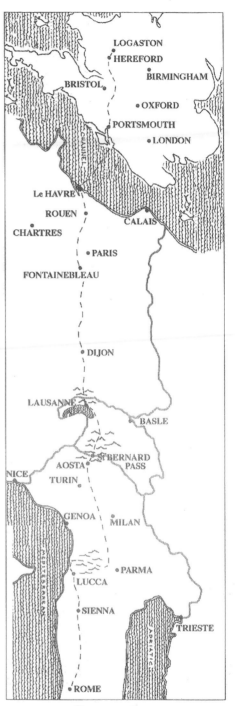

The route to Rome

List of Sponsors

* AIUK Charitable Trust and *The Friends and Supporters of St Owens Centre* can reclaim tax (28p for every £1 of sponsorship) if you are a UK tax payer and have paid enough income tax. All you need to do is tick the box (and give your name and address) and Amnesty International or The Friends of St Owens will do the rest.

Name	Address	Phone no/email (essential for gift aid)	Sponsoring Amnesty or St Owens Centre (please state which)	£ for 1,200 miles (or pro rata)	Gift Aid*
EXAMPLE J. Bloggs	*15 Footsore Close, Walker's Cramp, Herefordshire HR5 8ND*	*01989 340568*	*Amnesty*	*£12*	√

Cheques should be made out (for Amnesty) to 'Amnesty Rome Walk'
or (for the St Owens Centre) to 'Friends and Supporters of St Owens Centre'

About the St. Owens Centre

St. Owens Centre provides day care services for vulnerable adults with learning disabilities. About 22 operational staff members support between 43 to 50 people daily. They also act as drivers and escorts to the various activities. A majority of the people use wheelchairs and require specialist transport with tail lifts, and there are three vehicles used to get people to their voluntary work placements such as the 'Community cafe', charity shops and luncheon clubs led by WRVS.

Transport is also required for F.E. courses through the local colleges, community projects, such as recycling and waste management initiatives and therapy sessions associated with sensory development such as riding, reflexology and rebound therapy.

The Friends and Supporters of St Owens Centre Charity play a crucial role in the services and help towards lobbying and fund raising tasks. Currently, they are supporting our 'Mini bus appeal' towards replacing one of the vehicles through a sponsored walk.

Our website (www.fasoc.co.uk) now carries a form for the gift aid facility.

About Amnesty International

 Amnesty International is a movement of ordinary people from across the world standing up for humanity and human rights. Their purpose is to protect individuals where justice, fairness, freedom and truth are denied. They are totally independent of government and are free to point out abuses of power regardless of religion or political standpoint.

The Hereford, Leominster and Ludlow Group of Amnesty International (which is acting as collecting agent for the Amnesty sponsorship proceeds) has about 150 members who receive a local newsletter. The group holds an annual Street Collection in each of the three towns, and aims to send £2,000 a year to AIUK. They are also involved in Amnesty Campaigns, and have their own Group Prisoner of Conscience on whose behalf they campaign and write letters. New members are always welcome — if interested please contact Corinna, the Membership Secretary, on 01547 529786.

The printing of this form has been sponsored by PIP Printing, Aubrey Street, Hereford. Tel: 01432 344744

Pages from a Pilgrim Passport of this trip

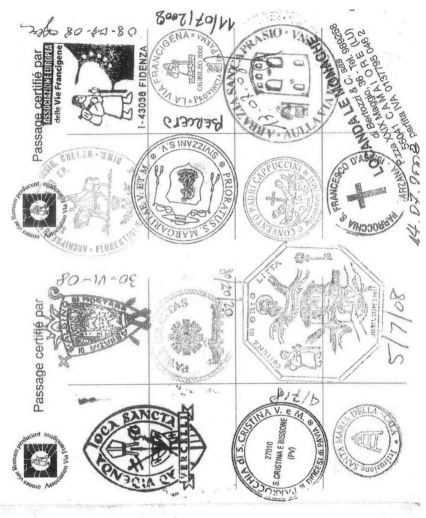

LITTERAE PATENTES

PEREGRINATORIS ITER PER VIAM

FRANCIGENAM FACIENTIS

PONTIFICIUM CONSILIUM
DE CULTURA

La Via Francigena "Major cultural route -
Grand itinéraire culturel du Conseil de l'Europe"

Best pizzas of the journey - cooked in a
transit van!

Even the Italian pilgrims sometimes lose
their way!

Spacious and luxurious...

Are we hallucinating?.... Maybe we shouldn't
have eaten those mushrooms?!